Snow Amazing

Cool Facts and Warm Tales

JANE DRAKE and ANN LOVE
Art by MARK THURMAN

Tundra Books

Dedication

This book is dedicated, with love, to our photographers –
Henry Barnett, Jim Drake, and David Love
J.D. and A.L.

To the crocus peeking through the snow
M.T.

Acknowledgments

The authors would like to thank Ruth Drake Alloway and Sam Alloway; Ian and Natalie Barnett; Kathleen and Henry Barnett; The Bowmanville Zoological Park, especially Michael Hackenberger, Wendy Korver, and Chris Vanderkooi; Trish Brooks; Jane Crist; Alex da Prado; Jim, Stephanie, Brian, and Madeline Drake; Tom and Emily Drake; Sara Drake; Ron Dueck; Stewart Elgie; Gilbert Flowers; Ruth Gotthardt; Dave, Matt, and Grant Gibson and the Balding Cres. road hockey team; Bob and Kathleen Lank; Mary Ann and Rob Lewis; Betty and Gage Love; David, Melanie, Jennifer, and Adrian Love; Joie Quarton; W.O. Pruitt; Luke and Olivia Love Racine; Mark Salmoni; Harold, Cindy, Melissa, and Aaron Smith; John Storey; and Rob Tuckerman.

A special acknowledgment to Joy Finlay, for her thoughtful and expert advice, and to Kristin Taylor, for her creative input.

Working with our publisher, Kathy Lowinger, is a delightful experience – she truly understands the close connection between snow and chocolate. Special thanks to our supportive and keen-eyed editor, Sue Tate, as well as the entire team at Tundra Books.

Text copyright © 2004 by Jane Drake and Ann Love
Art copyright © 2004 by Mark Thurman

Published in Canada by Tundra Books,
481 University Avenue, Toronto, Ontario M5G 2E9

Published in the United States by Tundra Books
of Northern New York,
P.O. Box 1030, Plattsburgh, New York 12901

Library of Congress Control Number: 2004100577

Medium: Watercolor and colored pencil on paper

Design: Cindy Reichle

This book is printed on acid-free paper that contains post-consumer waste.

National Library of Canada Cataloguing in Publication

Drake, Jane
    Snow amazing : cool facts and warm tales / Jane Drake, Ann Love ; art by Mark Thurman.

Includes index.
ISBN 0-88776-670-6

1. Snow–Juvenile literature. I. Love, Ann II. Thurman, Mark, 1948- III. Title.

QC926.37.D73 2004   j551.57'84   C2004-900492-1

We acknowledge the financial support of the Government of Canada through the Book Publishing Industry Development Program (BPIDP) and that of the Government of Ontario through the Ontario Media Development Corporation's Ontario Book Initiative. We further acknowledge the support of the Canada Council for the Arts and the Ontario Arts Council for our publishing program.

Printed in Canada

1 2 3 4 5 6   09 08 07 06 05 04

Table of Contents

Think Snow!

You jump out of bed on a midwinter morning, run to the window, and look out. Still no snow! It's the same view as yesterday – brown grass, fallen leaves, an idle snow shovel, and a quiet bird feeder.

You throw on a coat and step outside. A damp chill creeps up your back, so you warm up by hopping over the gray puddles on the sidewalk. When can you try out your new skis and throw a snowball? How long can plants, chipmunks, and salamanders survive the cold without a protective cover of snow? What will happen if there are no snowbanks to melt in the spring and water the soil? What if it never snows again? What if all the snow in the world vanishes? Will the seas really rise and flood whole cities? Will words like "snowman" and "snowmobile" disappear?

Next morning you awake to a deep quiet. Your ears feel plugged and you swallow hard. Then you glance out the window and there it is – snow! Tons of it blanket the ground, muffling all sound. Birds flit around the bird feeder; it's white everywhere, not a blade of grass in sight. What will you do when you get outside – stomp footprints all over the yard, find your flying saucer, start a snow fort? It's magical, it's fantastic, it's snow.

This book celebrates snow: from the formation of a snowflake to the snow adaptations of a caribou; from the danger of an avalanche to the thrill of a toboggan ride. Underneath the celebration is a healthy dose of respect. This book asks you to think about snow and how remarkable, valuable, and amazing snow really is!

Snow in the Forecast
Possibility of Snow

Step into your boots and out into the fresh snow. Is it up to your ankles? Walk down the steps and pull a shovel out from under a small snowdrift. By now, you've probably crushed, kicked, shoved, and brushed at least a million snow crystals. Imagine how many multi-trillions fall each year to Earth. Because each snow crystal forms and falls under changing conditions, it's unlikely you'll ever find two that are exactly alike.

A snow crystal is born

Each snow crystal starts as a minute fleck of dust drifting high above the ground. It could be a particle of soil lifted by the wind from a farmer's field, or a cinder blasted from deep inside a volcano. It could be a particle of smoke trailing from a forest fire, or an infinitesimal meteoroid falling from outer space.

The fleck enters a cloud of supercooled water vapor molecules and droplets ready to freeze the moment they touch anything solid. One collides with the fleck and together they form an ice crystal, a simple six-sided shape. This starts a tiny current of air that draws more water molecules towards the crystal, where some sublimate – or solidify. The crystal keeps sublimating water vapor until it becomes heavy enough to start falling to Earth. If it continues to fall through cold air and keeps growing, the ice crystal will finally be visible to the human eye. At that point, it is called snow.

As the crystal falls, it spins with its widest surface facing down. If it passes through cold moist air, it may pick up water vapor along its edges and grow long delicate rays. It may join with other snow crystals and create a snowflake, which, in a little wind, could smash

into other snowflakes and shatter. If it passes through even moister cold air, it may become so heavily coated with water droplets that it turns into an ice pellet, its crystal shape hidden inside. Or if it passes through a patch of warm air, it may fall as rain, disappear, or re-form later as a new ice crystal.

A snow crystal becomes part of life wherever it falls. If it lands on a bear's den, it may help seal out the winter's cold. If it falls on a slope, come spring it could water a farmer's crop downstream. If it drops onto a road, it may cause a driver to brake. If it settles on a glacier, over the years it could turn into fossil snow, worth studying by a future scientist. Or if it lands on a mountain, it may speed up a skier's down-hill glide. And then, one day, the snow crystal will melt and leave behind its fleck of dust.

Snow crystal shapes

Scientists agree that snow crystals can be sorted into a few basic shapes. Each depends on the temperature and moisture where it formed and the conditions through which it fell on its journey to the ground. In fresh snow, look for six-sided plates, prisms, stars, needles, columns, capped columns, and fernlike branches (dendrites) as well as irregular shapes.

In Today's Forecast – Snow!

"We have a severe weather warning in effect for the entire region. High winds, blowing snow, and accumulations up to 30 centimeters – that's about 12 inches. Road crews are ready to work round the clock. . . ."

Every winter's day, meteorologists predict how much snow will fall, when, and where. Although everyone complains when they get it wrong, weather forecasters are often right. So how do they predict?

Meteorologists start off by asking four questions. Are there enough water vapor molecules and flecks of dust in the atmosphere to form ice crystals? Is it below 0° C (32° F) in the layers of air through which the crystals will fall? Are the clouds deep enough so the crystals will grow as they drop? And is there sufficient moist air in the clouds to replace the water vapor that will turn into snow?

When a moist air mass is forced to rise at freezing temperatures, meteorologists often get the answer "yes" to their questions. So they watch for these kinds of conditions on a cold day:

• *Orographic Lift* – When moist air approaches a ridge, hills, or mountains, it has nowhere to go but up. As the air rises it expands, cools, and condenses to form clouds. If cold and unstable enough, snow will develop as the air rises up the slope.

• *Lake Effect* – When cold dry air flows over a large lake that remains unfrozen, the lake water warms and moistens the air immediately above it. Warm air is lighter than cold air, so the warmer moistened air rises, expands, and cools again to form fog or cloud. If the temperature is cold enough, snow may develop before the air flow reaches land.

• *Frontal Lift* – When a mass of cold air advances on a mass of warm air, the cold air, being heavier, undercuts the warm air and forces the warm air up. The leading edge of cold air is called a cold front. When a mass of warm air advances on a mass of cold air, the lighter warm air rises up and over the cold air. The leading edge of a warm air mass is called a warm front. In both cases, as the air rises, it cools and clouds form. If the clouds are cold and moist enough, snow will develop.

Meteorologists measure the speed, direction, and amount of water in the rising air. They double-check to be sure it is cold enough for snow – an extremely small change in temperature can mean the difference between snow and rain. Then they forecast how much and where snow will fall. With computers helping to take measurements and make predictions, they're usually, but not always, right.

Looks like snow

If you see clouds coming on a wintry day, sometimes you can tell what kind of snow they carry. Puffy, mounding cumulus clouds that are lumpy like cauliflower often form along an advancing cold front and bring snow showers. High, wispy cirrus clouds form ahead of an advancing warm front followed by stratus clouds – layered, low, and flat. Stratus clouds can bring continuous snow. The darker the cloud cover, the heavier the snowfall.

Why winter at all?

Every day, Earth spins one full circle on its axis, a line that runs from the North to the South Pole. The axis holds Earth at an angle to the Sun. And every year, Earth orbits around the Sun so that, on its axis, the North Pole tilts towards the Sun in summer and away from it in winter. That means energy from the Sun has farther to travel to reach north in winter than it does in summer. And that makes the north colder in winter and the chances greater that snow will fall instead of rain.

Snow on the Ground, Snow All Around

Skiers dream of deep powder snow. This luxury occurs when perfect crystal stars fall on a calm day at about −15° C (5° F). The crystals land with their tips interlocked, trapping lots of air and making the lightest, fluffiest snow cover possible. Usually, perfect snow crystals don't last long. The slightest breeze will break their delicate arms and a strong wind will reduce them to look-alike grains. Even if they land gently, snow crystals can be crushed by snow above, warmed by soil beneath, and compacted by gravity. Once they settle, the crystals, fragments, and grains bond together, where they touch, recrystallize, and harden in a process called sintering.

A fresh snowfall may soon look like a seamless blanket, but it's not. Snow on the ground is dynamic. It changes constantly, depending on wind, warmth, and moisture. Cut through an older snowbank and you'll find layers. The top layer may be powdery or crusty, while the middle layers may be granular or icy. The bottom layer is often warm, moist, and with loose sugary crystals – but not always. Sami herders of northern Europe describe the layer of snow that lies next to the soil with several different words. Their reindeer must dig through it to reach their preferred food – lichen. If the bottom layer is made up of fragile crystal columns, it is called *sändjas*, easy to brush away with a hoof. Frozen granular snow, or *bodni vihki*, is harder to dig into. A base of solid ice, or *cuok'ki*, may be impossible for a reindeer to break through. But worst of all is *caevvi*, hard dense snow that lies over unfrozen soil. Snow mold grows in *caevvi* and releases gases that prevent reindeer from smelling the lichen, so they don't even know where to dig for food.

Kovakmiut hunters of northwestern Alaska survive harsh subarctic winters because of their intimate understanding of ground snow. They have specific names for the many different kinds of drifts they encounter in travel. And when snow falls in a forest, it isn't just "snow" – it's named depending on where it falls and what kind of environment it creates. The Kovakmiut language is so rich in snow words that many ecologists today use it for precise scientific reporting.

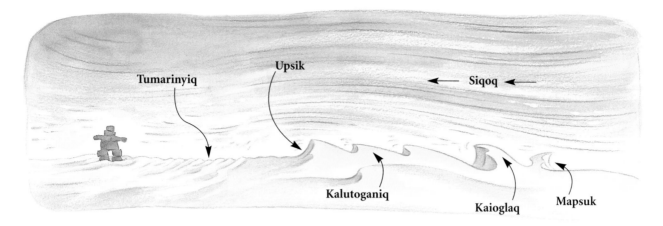

Kovakmiut words for windblown tundra snow

Siqoq – drifting or blowing snow

Upsik – wind-hardened tundra snow

Tumarinyiq – a very small ripple drift

Kalutoganiq – an arrowhead-shaped drift

Kaioglaq – the hard wind-sculpted remains of kalutoganiq

Mapsuk – an anvil-shaped drift

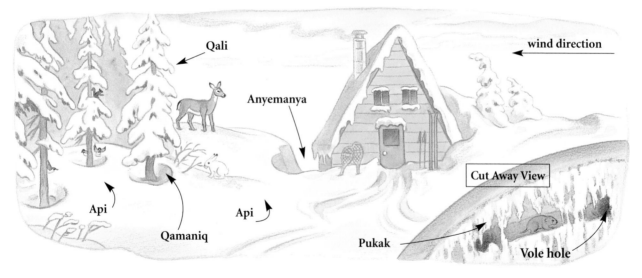

Kovakmiut words for settled forest snow

Api – snow on the ground

Qali – snow on the trees

Qamaniq – a bowl-shaped depression in the api under evergreen trees

Pukak – the base layer of api made up of hollow snow crystals shaped like rods and pyramids and arranged in columns

Anyemanya – the space formed between a drift and the obstruction causing it

Spring Thaw

You know spring is coming when Groundhog Day is over, hockey playoffs have started, and baseball fans are counting down to opening day. You can also tell winter is ending by looking at snow. Just before melt, the snowbanks suddenly seem shrunken, tired, and a little see-through. In the early morning, the snow feels crusty to walk on, and piles by the roadside are rock hard. On a windy day, there's not much loose fluffy snow to blow around.

These changes in the snow are caused by warming from the late-winter Sun. With longer days and more sunshine, the snow surface melts in daytime and refreezes at night, creating a crust. On the next sunny day, ice in the crust lets heat and light farther down into the snowbank and the following morning's crust will have deepened. Meanwhile, stronger rays from the Sun sublimate some of the surface snow into water vapor – the snow disappears right into the air. Over time, the snowbank slumps.

When the temperature of a snowbank rises to the melting point ($0°$ C or $32°$ F), a film of water covers the individual snow crystals and the pores between the crystals fill with water. As the Sun keeps heating up the bank, gravity pulls the water down into the soil below. Before long, downward draining channels form in the snowbank. If it refreezes overnight, the next morning's sunlight shines through the channels, making the snowbank look a little transparent and fragile, although it is actually hard until the Sun heats it up again.

The weeks, and sometimes months, it takes for all the snow to melt can be a stressful time for animals. Those that live and walk on the top of snow often get cuts on their legs breaking through the crust. When the surface turns wet in the Sun, travel in slush is difficult. Creatures that live in and under the snow suffer in the wet environment and can even get flooded out.

On the other hand, as the snow becomes more see-through, their dark underworld brightens and the first plants start to grow, some poking right through the snow.

For people, melting snow can cause dangerous travel and flooding. But we rely on the spring thaw. Many places in the world where grain and crops grow are watered by rivers fed with snowmelt. Same with the pastures our animals graze on and the forests we harvest.

Farmers time their planting according to the pattern of snowmelt. Sometimes they live where they can actually watch the melt and track which sunny hillsides become bare first and which north slopes and valleys hold snow the longest.

In Honshu, Japan, rice-growers keep their eye on the snow covering a nearby mountainside in early spring. When the last patch melts down to the shape of a man carrying a hoe, they know there will be enough water to plant their rice seedlings.

Legendary Snowmen

Every now and then, a scientist or artist becomes possessed by snow and studies it passionately. Here are the stories of three indomitable snowmen!

Snowflake Bentley

In 1885, at the age of nineteen, Wilson A. Bentley of Jericho, Vermont was the first person to photograph a snow crystal. He combined a camera with a microscope and shot his photomicrographs in a woodshed.

Mr. Bentley was a farmer, but snowflakes were his obsession. When snow fell without wind to damage the crystal shapes, he would drop everything, collect crystals on a wooden tray, and photograph them. He often retouched his prints to enhance their beauty. In 1931 he published a book of over 2,400 photographs – less than half of the 5,381 he took in his lifetime. And, as he pointed out, no two were identical.

That same year he caught a chill while outside collecting crystals and died soon after. But his images survive – an amazing record of exquisite, long-vanished snowflakes.

Professor Church

A Latin professor at the University of Nevada, Dr. James Church first climbed Mount Rose, outside Reno, on New Year's Eve in 1895. The only equipment he had to scale the 3,285 meter (10,778 ft.) peak were rubber boots and a pair of snowshoes.

The local power company was also interested in Mount Rose because its spring runoff watered the desert city. In 1906, Dr. Church offered to climb the summit every two weeks to collect data on the snowpack. The power company was enthusiastic, so Church arranged for horses to drag an instrument shed over the snow to the summit.

Dr. Church began his biweekly trips. Some climbs took several tries to get to the top. Once, he had to dig a trench in the snow partway up to survive howling winds and freezing temperatures. When he reached the shed the following morning, the door was frozen shut and he couldn't record anything. He returned to his trench and the next day tried again in thick fog and swirling snow. He couldn't see so he shouted and used his echo to find the way. When the fog lifted for a moment, he realized he was off course, so he slid back down to the trench. On the fourth morning, the day dawned clear and warm – perfect for scaling the summit and recording measurements.

Dr. Church invented a gauge to measure the water content of snow at different depths. His Mount Rose Snow Sampler was eventually used around the world to predict snow runoff.

Dr. Nakaya

Inspired by Bentley's photographs, Ukichiro Nakaya, a physicist at Hokkaido University in Japan, turned his scientific eye to snow crystals. He decided to catch, categorize, and measure as many as possible through every snowfall during the winter of 1932. Later, he reproduced in a laboratory most of the different kinds of natural snow crystals he found. A snow crystal, he discovered, is "a letter from the sky": information written on a crystal lets you read the weather above. He created a chart to help meteorologists predict atmospheric conditions by examining snow crystals that reach the ground.

Tciwetinowinu* – An Innu Legend

With thick frost-repellent coats, wolverines are well adapted to endure the severest winter cold. Although they have short legs, they can run quickly over deep snow on their big furry paws. To survive the harshest winters, wolverines are known to steal meat from wolf kills, or spring traps and snatch the bait. They will attack large animals and defend themselves with incredible ferocity. The Innu of Labrador respect wolverines. Tough, gutsy, and smart, Wolverine is their legendary trickster.

One winter Wolverine found he was wading through slush all the time. He sank in right up to his thighs, even along the trails. And he couldn't travel across rivers or lakes because they were either not frozen or there was too much water on top of the ice.

"What's the matter with you, Tciwetinowinu?" Wolverine called out to the weather god as he slogged through the slush. "Don't you know how to make a real winter?"

*pronounced *Chee-wet-innow-innew*

Farther down the trail, Wolverine met a giant dressed in white. "I am Tciwetinowinu," the giant said. "I hear you don't like the weather this winter."

"That's right," Wolverine replied. "I wish it were colder, with real snow – not this slush."

The giant grinned and said, "Well, I'll see what I can do."

The next winter started off warm again. Wolverine struggled once more through slush. But suddenly it turned very cold and snow fell in great flakes. It got so cold, in fact, that Wolverine's teeth chattered, and the snow was so thick it got into his mouth and eyes.

After a few days of this weather, the giant weather god walked into Wolverine's tent, grinned, and asked, "Is it cold and snowy enough for you now?"

Wolverine didn't like the way Tciwetinowinu enjoyed his power over the weather. He stoked up his fire with grease and refused to admit anything. "Actually," Wolverine said, "I was hoping it would be colder and snowier."

The next day it turned much colder and the snow came down in even larger flakes. The tree branches snapped under the weight of the snow. Wolverine's paws froze and he felt the cold deep inside his bones.

Tciwetinowinu visited Wolverine's tent again and asked if it was finally cold and snowy enough. Half-frozen and angry, Wolverine refused to answer. Instead, he started talking quickly, telling all the gossip he knew, while he poured more and more grease on his fire.

The giant sat down and listened to Wolverine's chatter without noticing the tent getting warmer. Suddenly he started to melt. He jumped up and cried, "Ah, you've tricked me! You've beaten me at my own game," and rushed outside into the frigid air and snow.

Ever since, winters have been winters – not too warm, not too cold, and with just the right amount of snow. Even so, the Innu always remember to pitch their tents facing south so that Tciwetinowinu will not be tempted to blow cold and snow in through the door.

Snow Wonders
Lights, Camera, Snow . . .

On a still, freezing cold morning when the Sun shines across the snow, the tips of weeds, shrubs, and evergreen needles sparkle in the sunlight. If a breeze ruffles through the trees, crystals sweep off the branches in light showers, hanging in the air like diamonds before sifting to the ground. At night, under a full Moon, the snow on the ground can be so bright that passing clouds cast shadows. And the underside of each cloud blinks with moonlight reflected off the snow.

Filmmakers know that snow and light create amazing, natural special effects, or SFX. In the Arctic, where snow covers much of the land and sunlight shines at low angles, the SFX are sensational.

FADE IN

EXTERIOR. ON A CLEAR LATE AFTERNOON, ST. BRENDAN AND SEVEN-TEEN IRISH MONKS SAIL IN THE NORTH ATLANTIC, SIXTH CENTURY – LONG SHOT

The MONKS, *in a long narrow open* BOAT *covered in ox hides, sail towards the horizon. No land in sight.*
ZOOM TO THE HORIZON – DISSOLVE

An ISLAND *appears above the horizon. It shimmers and looms, but its snow-covered hills and dark rocks are distinct.*
ZOOM OUT
ST. BRENDAN *raises his arms in surprise and wonder.*

When layers of warm air lie over a cold sea, the outgoing rays of the Sun can be refracted or bent back to Earth and create a mirage. Sometimes the layers line up like lenses in a telescope and can magnify distant snow-covered headlands, creating images that make them look closer than they really are. Today, if conditions are right, sailors northwest of Scotland get glimpses of the snowy peaks of Iceland – then Greenland, then Labrador – when they are too far away to see any land. Is it possible that early European sailors ventured to the New World because they had already seen its shores?

CUT TO

EXTERIOR. A SAILING BRIG, FROZEN IN ICE OFF MELVILLE ISLAND, 1820

   On deck, LIEUTENANT WILLIAM PARRY, *age twenty-nine, in full British naval winter uniform, sketches his view of the sky on* PAPER *with* PEN.
ZOOM OUT

   Parry and his ship diminish in the huge arctic snowscape. The blue sky is veiled by thin cirrus clouds. The Sun, just above the horizon, is surrounded by a giant halo with sun dogs on either side, shining red closest to the Sun, yellow in the middle, and blue farthest away from the Sun.

Lieutenant William Parry measured and recorded all the spectacular arcs, halos, and sun dogs he observed in the arctic sky. Like other sailors, he expected snow within a day or two of seeing these brilliant splashes of light. He didn't know the effects occur when sunlight hits short six-sided pencil-shaped ice crystals about 10,000 meters (33,000 ft.) above

ground, which may or may not grow large enough to fall as snow.

CUT TO

EXTERIOR. ON AN OVERCAST DAY, AN INUIT HUNTER STALKS A POLAR BEAR ACROSS SNOW AND EXPOSED ROCKS, EARLY TWENTIETH CENTURY – LONG SHOT

   Wearing a skin parka, RIFLE *in hand, the* HUNTER *leaves his* SLED *and* DOGTEAM *and creeps forward towards the* BEAR.
ZOOM IN ON BEAR – DISSOLVE

   The bear suddenly shrinks into a MARMOT *and dives into its den in the rocks.*
FADE OUT

On dull winter days, when the only colors are white and black, the human eye finds it hard to judge size and distance. A marmot can be mistaken for a bear, or a bear for a marmot. Inuit people are well acquainted with tricks to the eye in the arctic air. They say that Sila, powerful spirit of the weather and the atmosphere, produces these wonders.

Snow Sense

Snow attacks the senses. It feels cold, but can burn the skin; it's freezing cold, yet a fantastic insulator; it falls silently, but can squeak when you step on it; it's usually odorless, but can give off the summer fragrance of watermelon. Most would agree that snow looks white, but through the eyes of an artist, snow runs the full spectrum of colors.

When Kristin, an art student, prepares to paint a snow scene, she tosses aside the idea that snow is white. In her mind, she breaks down all the surfaces. Shades of white compose the base color, but there are highlights of yellow, orange, and pink and shadows of purple, violet, and blue. She's aware that the snow is covering objects below it, and like an iceberg above water, what's below the surface determines the shape and color of the whole.

Depending on the density of the snow and what it's hiding, light is absorbed to different depths and can reflect back a variety of hues. Kristin will use these subtle color variations to contour and form the scene. She'll create a mood by her color choices – blasting arctic air at her viewers with cold whites, blues, and purples, or luring them outdoors with warm whites, yellows, and pinks. And Kristin will paint snow as it exists within a habitat by adding hints of color from the surroundings, such as trees, sky, and rocks.

Like gently falling snow, painting this scene takes time and will have many layers. Using a technique called glazing, she'll build up thin coatings of paint. Light and color will travel through the paint until Kristin's snow shimmers.

Sounds like snow

Military scientists studying the effects of rain on submarine sonar equipment made an accidental discovery about snow. A snowflake melts when it lands on water, at the same time trapping some air underwater. The air immediately surfaces and pops, making a high-pitched shriek that the human ear cannot hear.

Snow Prints

Imprints left in the snow are like moments frozen in time, revealing everything from daily routines and action-packed adventures to gruesome dramas. Depth and spacing of prints, feathers, tufts of fur, bones, seed cases, scat, urine, and blood all provide clues of who was there, when, and what happened. And snow prints can lead to the den door.

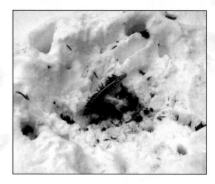

Snowy Owl and Mouse

Gliding low on the silent air of a cold winter evening, the snowy owl spies a mouse nibbling a twig in the shadows where trees meet meadow. Close to the target, one wing brushes the top few crystals off the light coating of new snow. Thrusting forward with his talons, the owl misjudges the contours of a drift and pitches face first into a fluffy, feathered pile. The mouse bolts for cover as the very snowy owl bounces forward and swivels his neck to the rear (see cover). Snowy owls are master hunters on tundra, where snow is hard and thin. When hunger forces them south, they struggle with deep, wet, or powdery meadow snow.

Red Fox and Field Mouse

Keen nose to the wind, the red fox trots lightly across a farmer's field. She slows and listens at a snowbank. Hearing nothing, she squirts out a bit of urine and continues hunting. Her feet, as big as a medium-sized dog's, leave a nearly straight track across the snow. When she senses movement beneath the surface, she rises up on her hind legs and pounces down hard with her front paws. Underneath the snow crust, a worn tunnel collapses. Another well-placed pounce seals the rodent in a living tomb. Now the fox digs ferociously and pulls out her meal. A few drops of blood, fur, and footprints will be all that remains.

Brown Rat

Tiny prints crisscross the garden. They look like a child's drawing of a setting sun, with five toes on the back feet and four on the front. Some prints lead to the recycling box, others to the base of the bird feeder. Before last night's snow, several sets of prints – complete with dragging tail marks – lead to the composter. If you're brave enough to lift the lid, don't be surprised if a family of brown rats leap out. They know that compost is warm in the dead of winter. The rotting process creates heat, and the new snow covering the box helps insulate the rats from the cold.

Bear

The creature must be large. The prints sink deep into the soft spring snow – looking nearly human, but wider and with obvious claws. Whatever it was, stopped by the lake, maybe for a drink or the chance of a fish. It walked on all fours to the big spruce tree and clawed it about a meter off the ground. Then, just before its tracks went back into the thicket, it left behind a large cylinder of scat. The dark, brown deposit sank into the snow, absorbing heat from the sun and melting the surrounding snow.

Deer

Seasoned naturalists can tell how long ago a deer passed by. The arrow-shaped print of a deer's hoof has the same hardness as the snow around it for about an hour. Then it begins to get crusty, starting from the top of the print and then down into the base. After a day or two, the prints are frozen solid and the deer is long gone.

Snow Monsters

Show us the Sasquatch!

WANTED: REPORTER/PHOTOGRAPHER WITH SENSE OF ADVENTURE AND WILDERNESS SURVIVAL SKILLS. KNOWLEDGE OF CRYPTOZOOLOGY (STUDY OF UNKNOWN ANIMALS) AN ADVANTAGE, BUT NOT A NECESSITY. MUST BE DETERMINED, LEVELHEADED, AND STEADY ARMED. YOUR EDITOR WILL NOT ACCEPT THE FOLLOWING EXCUSES: NO FILM, DEAD BATTERIES, NO FLASHLIGHT, BAD WEATHER, SHAKY CAMERA, OR FAINTING FROM FRIGHT. WE REQUIRE THE FIRST SASQUATCH PHOTOGRAPH OF THE NEW MILLENNIUM — WITHOUT DIGITAL ENHANCEMENT — ACCOMPANIED BY A DETAILED ACCOUNT OF YOUR SIGHTING. ONLY SERIOUS APPLICANTS NEED APPLY. NO PRACTICAL JOKERS PLEASE.

Since Norseman Leif Ericson reported seeing a huge hairy monster with black eyes in 986 A.D., there have been thousands of Bigfoot or Sasquatch sightings in North America. Some have been deliberate hoaxes, some possible dreams or mystic encounters. Others have left scientists scratching their heads. Details vary, but a general profile of the creature has emerged. It is above normal human height, hairy, solitary, smells foul, leaves behind enormous droppings and footprints, walks upright while swinging its arms, slouches, and has an apelike face. No province or state has been left unvisited, but it is most frequently spotted in the northwestern U.S. and Canada. Sasquatches are everywhere and nowhere.

Sasquatch habitat is remote, wild, and often mountainous. While fewer sightings occur in winter, it is thought that these elusive creatures do not hibernate but forage for buds and tree bark, as do winter-active porcupines, moose, and elk. Curious woodsmen have followed big footprints in the snow from one cluster of trees to another, with a telltale trail of balsam twigs left behind. One such trail went into a snow cave at the heel of a glacier. Only a thick-furred creature would call that home. A certain cryptozoologist thought they could be migratory in nature, moving up and down the West Coast with the seasons. Another observer wondered if Sasquatch collect and store fruit, nuts, and berries for winter meals.

With nothing but plaster casts of footprints and a few blurry pictures to support their existence, we don't know if Sasquatch are alive, ever lived, or are now extinct. But, one late-winter day, Natalie Barnett had a fleeting glance of a large, hairy, obviously female creature standing on two legs at the edge of the

Thompson River in B.C. She caught a whiff of a disgusting odor before the creature crashed through the bushes out of sight. The shoreline was covered with over-sized footprints.

Abominable Snowmen

Bigfoot or Sasquatch could have originated in Asia, home of the Yeti or Abominable Snowman. Some cryptozoologists think they crossed the Beringian land bridge during the last ice age. Yeti – described as smaller versions of Sasquatch – are said to live at high elevations in Nepal, Tibet, and the Himalayas of India.

The Little Snow Girl – A Russian Folktale

At just the right temperature, snow can be made into sculptures that look almost real. In this Russian folktale, a snow sculpture actually comes to life.

An old man and his wife lived in a cozy home at the edge of a village, close to the forest. They had all they needed – a vegetable garden, chickens, a cow, and hunting dogs – just a few steps from their front door, and they were in the company of good neighbors. Despite all this, the old woman and man were unhappy. They were never blessed with children.

After finishing her chores on a winter's day, the old woman sat by the window and watched the local children run past her door, pulling their sleds, laughing and throwing snowballs in the air. Her husband saw the longing in his wife's face and felt sad, too. One day he said, "Come, let's make a little daughter out of snow."

The snow was just right for rolling, packing, and patting. With tender hands, they formed a little girl, complete with bonnet, smock, and apron. She looked like a real child except that her eyes were blank and her cheeks and lips were icy white.

The old woman said to the little snow girl, "You are more beautiful than a birch tree in spring. If only you could laugh and run like the other children."

With that, the snow girl's eyes flashed bright blue, her lips and cheeks blushed pink, her hair turned black and bounced as she started dancing in the snow.

At first, the old man and woman stared in wonder. But when the little snow girl held out her hands, the old man and woman each

• 26 •

took one and they danced together in the yard until nightfall. In a musical voice, clear as glass bells, the little snow girl said, "I will stay with you as long as you love me, but I must spend the nights outdoors so that I never get too warm."

That night, the little snow girl played outside the kitchen door in the moonlight, chasing her shadow in the snow. The old woman stayed up late, stitching a light coat from a blanket, and the old man went to a neighbor with a ruble to buy a fur hat and boots.

The next morning, the little snow girl ate a bowl of crushed ice for porridge, put on her new clothes, and ran to play with the village children in the snow. Of all of them, she ran the fastest, threw snowballs the farthest, and danced the longest. When the children made a snowman, she joined in with her merry tinkling laugh. She was so much fun to be with that the other children couldn't imagine playing without her. The old woman watched with pride from the window. In the evening, the snow girl ate another bowl of crushed ice and then played by the kitchen door, throwing snowballs at the northern lights.

And so it went all winter long. The village children came every day to ask her to play. The old man and his wife were so happy.

As spring approached, the paths became clearer and the children took their games into the forest. One day, the little snow girl danced so far ahead of the others, she got lost. Her friends looked and looked, but had to return home as darkness fell. Deep in the forest, the little snow girl climbed a tree and called for help.

A big brown bear, just awake from his winter's sleep, heard her and growled, "Come down and I will take you home, my dear." But the little snow girl was afraid and stayed in her tree.

Later, a gray wolf stopped by and offered to help. But the little snow girl said, "No, thanks. I am waiting for someone else."

When a red fox passed nearby, she called out and asked him to walk her home. The fox agreed and told her to grab the fur on his back while he led her out of the forest.

Meanwhile, back in the village, the old couple feared the worst. The old woman cried by the fire and the old man stood beside her, unable to offer comfort.

Suddenly they heard their little snow girl calling outside, "Tie up the dogs. A kind fox has brought me home."

The old man joyfully shut away his hunting dogs and threw open the door, welcoming them into the house. The old woman thanked the fox and threw him a crust of bread.

The fox said, "I've been hungry for many nights. I would love a plump chicken to eat. Your little girl is worth more than a crust, is she not?"

"Of course," the old woman replied. But when she and her husband went outside to get the chicken, she said, "We have our little girl back now. The fox doesn't need one of our chickens."

So they found two bags and put a chicken in one and a hunting dog in the other. Then they called the fox to join them outside. The old woman let the chicken out of one bag and, before the fox could lick his lips, the old man

let the dog out of the other. The fox saw the dog's eyes flash in the dark just in time. The old man and woman watched the fox run for its life, back to the forest, without their chicken.

Then they heard the little snow girl calling inside the house in her clear musical voice, "Good-bye, good-bye. I will not stay when you love me less than a chicken."

As the old man and woman ran back into the house, they felt a cold wind blow past them. On the floor they found her blanket coat, fur hat, and boots beside a small puddle of water. Their little daughter of snow had left to play and dance where she had come from, under the stars in the Far North.

One day she may return and bring happiness to another childless couple. And they may love her more than their chickens.

Snow Power
Avalanche!

"What flies without wings, strikes without hands, and sees without eyes?"

– An old riddle

Stan McLennan thought he had the best job in the world. His wife was cook and he was manager of a promising gold mine on a mountainside above Ben-My-Chree in northwestern British Columbia. Each morning, exhilarated by the fresh mountain air, he strode from his cabin to the mine head, past wild and spectacular views of a huge glacier, blue-green lakes, and stark mountain peaks.

Before noon on a blue-sky October day in 1911, Stan ordered a round of shots be fired to loosen rock in an underground tunnel. While the miners set up for the blast, he walked across the snow to join his wife, Annie, who was preparing lunch. Standing in the cookhouse, Stan heard the shots ring out and then a low *whumph*. He did not see a crack appear in the snow above the tunnel, or the snow slab below the crack start sliding downhill. As the avalanche gained speed, it cut through the cookhouse but left untouched an outhouse on one side and a wood-pile on the other. One of the miners survived by riding on top, but Stan and Annie were buried in the snow. When their bodies were found, Annie was holding a potato and Stan a paring knife.

Worldwide, a million avalanches a year thunder down mountain slopes. Most occur in remote rugged regions, far from people. However, every winter there are snow adventurers, travelers, and workers who are caught and die in avalanches. Their lungs fill with snow powder, their chests are crushed by the weight of snow, or they run out of oxy-  gen. And these people themselves often trigger the avalanches that kill them.

Some avalanches are just small sloughs of loose surface snow that settle harmlessly. The serious killer avalanches are often large slabs of snow that start sliding

downhill in one piece.
When a slab avalanche is
over, a distinct crack line is
visible at the top. The crack
reaches down into a weak
layer – usually wet or loose-
grained snow – inside the
snowpack. When the weight
of the slab is greater than the
strength of its weakest layer,
the slab slides over that layer
until it gets going so fast that
nothing can stop it. In hazardous conditions, the weight
of one skier added to the
slab, or the vibrations of one
rifle shot shattering snow
crystals in the weak layer, can
unleash a killer slab avalanche.

Looking across a mountain slope, it's hard to tell if, hidden under the snow surface, there are dangerously weak layers. Travelers must look for warning signs, the most obvious being recent avalanches on nearby slopes. Fresh heavy snowfall, recent blowing snow, wet snow, marked warming, snow overhangs, and rain all increase avalanche danger.

Skiers, snowboarders, snowmobilers, and others who cross backcountry mountainsides should travel in groups with expert guides. Everyone should carry a radio transceiver so, if buried, others can locate them quickly. Travelers should also carry a portable shovel in case they have enough wiggle room to dig them-selves out, or need to dig a friend out. The other piece of essential equipment is a probe, which is helpful for prodding the snow and finding a buried victim alive. Perhaps if the miners at Ben-My-Chree had been better equipped, Stan and Annie would have survived.

Glaciers

A soft breeze parts Hans' white hair as he waits beside a gravel airstrip near Silver City, Yukon. Although it's clear and warm where he's sitting, the mountains to the south are cloud covered. The pilot won't fly him there until the visibility improves. But Hans doesn't mind the delay – he knows the danger of landing on a glacier in the best of conditions. After all, he once fell down a hidden crevasse and survived only because of the quick action of a friend. They had been tied together with a long rope and, when Hans disappeared, his friend drove her axe into the ice and wrapped her end of the rope around the axe handle. Already in free fall, Hans jerked to a stop. He dangled between gray-blue walls of ice. Below, all he could see was darkness. With the help of the steady rope, the crampons on his boots, and encouraging calls from above, he climbed up to the surface and survived. Since then, he has returned every summer to photograph and study the glacier and its many gaping crevasses.

Snow motion

Glaciers form in places where snow remains on the ground year-round – in parts of the Arctic, the Antarctic, and on high mountain slopes in between. Under the right glacier-making conditions, older snow is buried under fresh snow, year after year. The weight of snow slowly builds until the lower layers are crushed and compressed into ice. If the snow keeps accumulating, over hundreds and thousands of years, the ice gets thicker and thicker. Once it reaches about 18 meters (60 ft.) thick, the glacier becomes so heavy it starts to flow slowly down-hill, across plains, and, in some cases, into the sea. Like a hulking bulldozer, a glacier gouges, scratches, drags, and shoves everything in its way. If big enough, it can cut deep valleys, polish rock walls, and grind boulders to dust.

While you usually can't see a glacier move, you can see evidence of its moving. It carries and pushes rocky debris, or moraines, in long bands down its length and across its toe, or terminus. The strain of movement can also be seen in the giant crevasses that crack along the ice, especially where the glacier fans out or makes a small change in direction. At times you can even hear the sounds of a glacier moving – grinding, cracking, snapping, and groaning – especially when a glacier calves into icebergs, where it meets the sea.

As a glacier grows, with fresh snow accumulating at the upper end, it can advance or retreat far down at the bottom end, depending on the conditions there. Occasionally a glacier will surge forward several meters a day for weeks, or even months. Glaciologists study why they surge because, if all the glaciers in Antarctica and Greenland surged into the sea at once, sea levels around the world would rise dramatically, swamping coastal cities, farmlands, and forests.

Fossil snow

In Greenland, the glaciers are so thick, the snow-turned-ice at the very bottom can be thousands of years old. Glaciologists drill down and pull up core samples that read like tree rings – each layer reaching farther into the past. They study pollen grains, bacteria, and dust from the original ancient snow crystals and learn about plants, disease, and volcanoes in the times of woolly mammoths and saber-toothed tigers.

Snow in the Ice Age

The Innu tell the story of a man and his wife who, one snowy winter, went into the forest to collect wood. They made so much noise cutting that they woke a sleeping long-nosed beast. The giant creature charged and trampled them to death. Then it ate them and, with its tusk, tossed away their newborn son, Tchakapesh.

When they didn't return home, their daughter went looking for them. She  found only Tchakapesh, put him in a kettle, and fed him animal grease. In three days he grew to manhood and declared he was going to kill the beast that ate their parents.

Tchakapesh crafted a great bow from a birch sapling and arrows from a grove of spruce. His sister suggested he sew clothes for the battle, but Tchakapesh said, "The beast is naked, so I'll be naked too."

Tchakapesh stood in one of the creature's footprints in the snow and called out, "Come fight, you overgrown muskrat!"

Enraged, the beast charged. It threw Tchakapesh against a tree and bellowed, "How do you breathe through that puny thing on your face?" Tchakapesh shot an arrow into the beast's trunk and asked, "How do you breathe through that overgrown nose?"

The beast roared and charged again. The young man shot an arrow into its heart, killing it instantly. Tchakapesh made a mattress from its ears, a rope with its tail, and a paddle from its ribs. But every time he tried to eat its flesh, the meat grew wings and flew away. His sister touched the creature's severed head, which bounced around on the ground until Tchakapesh had to kill it again. They buried the head and that was the end of the giant long-nosed beast.

Is the giant beast in this story from eastern Canada a prehistoric mastodon, or even a woolly mammoth? In western Canada, the Gwich'in tell stories of a hero who killed an enormous, man-eating beaver by hammering its teeth into its mouth. Tagish storytellers recount the adventures of Beaverman, who traveled down the Yukon River killing giant lynx, bear, mink, and wolverine. Beaverman then taught their surviving young to stay small and, in that way, made the world safer for people. Do these stories explain the huge bones found now and then in the north? Or are they old memories from when humans hunted now-extinct giant mammals?

When the ice age ended about ten thousand years ago, the great glaciers that once covered much of Canada, western Asia, and Europe disappeared and so did the woolly mammoth, giant beaver, American lion, giant short-faced bear, and other fascinating oversized creatures. These mammals never lived right on the glaciers, but in the cold ice-free lands beside and in front of them. These lands tended to be dry-grass country, with thin snow cover in winter. As the glaciers melted, the atmosphere became moister as well as warmer, producing increased snowfall. Birch and spruce forests crowded out many of the grasslands and winter snows accumulated deeper. Scientists think the great mammals were overhunted by humans, who had developed sharper, more powerful weapons. But the giant beasts may have been easier prey, poorly adapted for foraging in forests or running away in deep snow.

Even with the advantage of deep, forest snow, killing an elephant-sized mastodon or mammoth would be a feat worth telling for thousands of years. As would hunting a beaver the size of a black bear, a ferocious American lion, or a long-legged, giant short-faced bear.

Snowbound: The Franklin Expedition

Excerpts from a fictional young man's diary tell the story of the Franklin Expedition, a chilling tale of men cut off and trapped by snow and ice.

May 19, 1845 – Today Sir John Franklin sailed from London to chart and conquer the snowy reaches of the Northwest Passage. His sturdy ships, the *Terror* and the *Erebus*, carry over three years of provisions, including 33,300 lbs. of meat preserved in tin cans and 9,260 lbs. of lemon juice to stave off scurvy. Dockside, amid the calls of crewmen working sails and ropes, I heard the bark of Neptune, the expedition dog, but did not see Jacko, the monkey . . .

April 4, 1850 – Three search expeditions have returned with no news of the 129 brave officers and seamen or their ships. Sir John's provisions will be exhausted. Her Majesty's government has posted a £20,000 reward for rescue of ships and men . . .

October 13, 1850 – Sir John's first winter quarters have been found on Beechey Island! There may yet be clues to the expedition's whereabouts. Captain Penny discovered three graves. Odd so many died the first winter out . . .

October 28, 1854 – Our worst fears are realized! John Rae of the Hudson's Bay Company met native hunters who told him that, some years ago, they traded seal meat for silverware with white men dragging lifeboats down the snow-covered west coast of King William Island. The hunters said they later found bodies farther south on the mainland, amid the bones of snow geese. Rae bought forks and spoons belonging to Captain Crozier of the *Erebus* from the hunters . . .

September 30, 1859 – Captain McClintock (head of the final search mission) found two notes inside a cairn on King William Island. One, dated 1847, stated the ships had overwintered in ice in Victoria Strait and all was well. The second, written around the edges of the first, dated April 25, 1848, reported Sir John had died the previous June. His ships had been trapped in ice for nineteen months. The surviving 105 men planned to walk south, looking for open water and rescue. So sad a tale told in so few words.

On the south shore, McClintock found a skeleton, in officer's uniform, and nearby, a clothes-brush, a comb, and a notebook, but alas no readable message! Inland, McClintock came upon two skeletons in a lifeboat along with guns, slippers, books, toothbrushes, tea, and chocolate. Weighing 1400 lbs. without cargo, the boat would have been incredibly heavy to drag, even over snow.

What those souls must have suffered, cut off for so long from home and family by snow and ice and cold. We know their fates years after they were long dead. . . .

Postscript

Scientists and adventurers are still searching for Franklin's lost ships. Expeditions had overwintered in the Arctic before – why did the best outfitted of all time fail? It was probably a mixture of causes:

• Unknowingly, Franklin chose the wrong route around King William Island. Pack ice on Victoria Strait does not always melt, even in warm summers.

• The British Navy scorned Inuit fur clothing made for survival in dry cold and snow. Instead, their men wore uniforms suitable for warmer, damp England.

• Climate experts believe the north was in a short ice age in Franklin's time, much colder and snowier than it is today.

• In 1986, Dr. Owen Beattie tested bone fragments from King William Island and hair from the graves. He found high levels of lead. Beattie suggested the tin cans – at the time a new technology for preserving food – may have been improperly sealed so that the lead used on the outside of the cans seeped into the contents. Lead poisoning would have weakened the men physically as well as mentally. Worst of all, it would have clouded their ability to make good decisions in dangerous snowbound conditions.

Blizzards – The Ultimate Snowstorms

WARNING . . . WINTER STORM WATCH IN EFFECT THIS EVENING . . . BITTER COLD, SEVERE WINDCHILL, BLOWING DRIFTING SNOW . . . POLICE SAY STAY HOME.

Blizzards are extreme and dangerous winter storms. Unlike ordinary snowfalls, blizzards have high winds and cold temperatures. And sometimes, it is not even snowing. The wind can whip up light, newly fallen snow, creating blizzard conditions. Some places are geo-graphically blizzard prone. Early settlers had no idea the lee of the Great Lakes would pro-duce snow bursts – sudden blinding blizzards that can be as small as a city block. The worst  blizzards happen where there is no windbreak from trees. And with nothing to stop the wind, blizzards can blow anywhere from three hours to ninety days.

In 1870, an Iowa journalist first called a wild snowstorm a blizzard. Before that, the word "blizzard" commonly described a round of musket fire. Sometimes as deadly as gunshots, high winds, poor visibility, and bone-numbing cold make blizzards hazardous for the millions of North Americans who battle them yearly.

Blizzards of the Centuries

1888

With the might of a cyclone, the blizzard of '88 rampaged up the eastern seaboard of North America for three days, paralyzing New York City, sinking over two hundred ships, and killing over four hundred people. A sopping wet warm air storm from Georgia and an arctic freeze gusting in from the west met over Manhattan. The resulting blizzard piled up record drifts that reached the second story of many apartment buildings and buried trains. Sleighs and carts were abandoned on snow-clogged streets. Civic workers couldn't shovel fast enough and even tried burning holes through the snow.

1977

On January 31, 1977, satellite images showed snow falling over all the continental U.S. and most of Canada. But in Buffalo, visibility was zero, with wind howling like a hurricane, making the air feel −51° C (−60° F). Schools closed as drifts climbed to twenty feet high. Some kids didn't make it home and spent the night at school. It took a week to dig out Buffalo, and once the plows were through, snow was piled as high as the electric wires along the roadsides.

The Big Snow in the Northland – A Dogrib Story

Before people lived on Earth, a community of fish, birds, and animals thrived along the shores of Great Slave Lake. No creature ate meat – they all lived together in peace.

One night, a great darkness swallowed up the lake and snow began falling, thick and deep. High winds came and the storm became a raging blizzard, burying all the plants. Many creatures died of starvation before the Chief called an emergency council meeting of all Earth animals. "We must send messengers to the Sky World. Sky creatures will know when the snow will stop and sunshine will return," he suggested.

The Chief and one animal from each species flew on the backs of birds up through a gateway to the Sky World and entered a magnificent lodge. Inside, three Sky bear cubs waited for their mother, Black Bear. She had gone by canoe to hunt Sky caribou. Earth's caribou became extremely nervous, but joined the rest of the visitors for a tour of the lodge.

High in the rafters hung five bags. Fox asked what was in them, but the Sky bear cubs refused to answer. Mother Black Bear had left them guarding the bags.

Now the Earth creatures were very curious. What secrets did the bags hold? Could they help the Great Slave Lake community?

Finally the biggest cub pointed to the closest bag and said, "That one's full of wind. The next one holds all the rain. The frosty one is the cold. That one's only fog." But he stopped and looked at the highest bag. The youngest cub piped up,

"If we tell you what's in that one, our mother will be angry."

The Chief of the Great Slave Lake creatures called his group outside for another council meeting. They could see Mother Black Bear canoeing back towards shore. The Chief said, "The last bag must be sunshine. I have a plan to get it." After hearing the whispered plans, all the creatures hid except Mouse, Caribou, and Fox, who were ready for action.

As Mother Black Bear walked towards the Sky World lodge, Mouse sprinted to the beached canoe and chewed across the handle of her paddle. As soon as the paddle was weakened, Mouse waved to Caribou,

who jumped into the water and swam out. Fox shouted to the cubs, "Your mother won't kill an Earth caribou, will she?" The cubs hollered to Mother Black Bear, empty-handed from her hunt, "There's a caribou, in the lake!" Mother Black Bear leapt back into her canoe and paddled madly towards Caribou. Her powerful strokes snapped the paddle in two, flipping the canoe. She plunged below the surface and was never seen again in the Sky World.

The Earth creatures jumped out of hiding and raced into the lodge. They pulled down the highest bag and hauled it to the gateway between the two worlds. Far below on Earth, even the tallest trees were buried in snow. When they dumped sunshine through the gateway, the snow melted quickly. But the big blizzard had changed things. And soon after, when humans arrived on the shores of Great Slave Lake, the old life was gone forever. Like humans, some creatures became carnivores, hunting and eating other animals.

Snow Alive
<u>Snow Bugs</u>

A snowball made with early spring snow – soft and grainy – isn't white. If you dissect that snowball, don't be surprised to find micro-bits of dust, droppings, plant debris, algae, exhaust particles, even meteorites peppered between the snow crystals. But, you probably aren't expecting "bugs."

Snow worms spend their lives on and in snow. Springtails (also called snow fleas) are tiny wingless insects that use a lever in their abdomens to catapult into the air. They flick around on snow, warmed by their black bodies that absorb solar energy and radiant heat from the snow. Snow worms and springtails eat algae and pollen off the surface of the snow and are welcome winter protein for spiders and birds.

Fortunately for snowball makers and eaters, not many insects remain active in snow. The cold and windy conditions that go hand in hand with snow limit insect food supply and make movement, growth, and reproduction nearly impossible. When the first snowstorm hits, you might find a dead bee or fly, but insects are usually long gone. The vast majority spend winter in a dormant or hibernating state. Many are protected as eggs; some are pupae. Select species – such as monarch butterflies – migrate, avoiding snow and cold altogether. The rest live through winter as adults. No matter where or how insects spend the winter, they're prepared in advance, avoiding or using snow to their advantage.

Insects need shelter from predators as well as protection from weather. Eggs are laid in or under tree bark, below ground, in leaf litter, inside nuts such as acorns, in the cocoons of other insects, or within the stems of plants. The female praying mantis builds a fortress for her eggs called an ootheca. It houses hundreds of eggs and is rock hard by midwinter. Ideally, wherever insect eggs are laid, they are then covered with fluffy, light snow. The snow insulates them from the wind and hides them from predators.

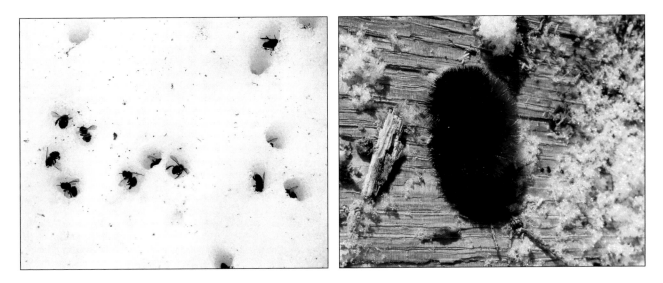

In fall, adult insects burrow into clumps of moss, mounds of grasses, or rotting logs. Ladybugs gather in large groups – as many as thousands – under rocks or in tree stumps and hibernate. When these hiding spots are sealed beneath a deep snowbank, they are insulated from the freezing air above the snow. The insects under the snow are not active and can appear dead, but most warm up and carry on living when spring comes. If there's no snow blanket, or if weather conditions are unusually harsh, large numbers of insects can perish.

Some northern insects freeze solid for the winter. One way they prepare their body tissues for freezing is by not eating, or by deliberately dehydrating. Also, some have antifreeze (called cryoprotectant) in their blood that lowers the temperature at which they freeze.

Plants and Snow

Some plants tough out winter weather with the help of special adaptations; others avoid snow, ice, and wind altogether by retreating underground. Migration is not an option, but many plants survive winter as seeds. Blizzards are deadly for some plants, drying and shredding leaves and snapping tender shoots. That's one reason why trees and shrubs shed their leaves in fall, withdrawing valuable nutrients to the protected core of the plant. Whichever way they deal with snow and cold, most plants are dormant – similar to hibernating – for the winter months.

• *Lichen* is one of the hardiest plants on Earth. It can survive being frozen solid, whipped by wind, and covered in snow. Starving arctic explorers eat one variety, called rock tripe. When certain types of lichen are covered with snow, they hug the damp ground or rock, and give off a distinct smell.

• Berry-bearing plants often hold on to their fruit well into the winter. *Snowberry shrubs* have white waxy berries that are an important winter food for woodland birds. Seeds sink into the snow with bird droppings, ready to germinate in the spring. *Highbush cranberries* are not eaten in the fall, but gobbled up in late winter by hungry flocks of birds, such as Bohemian waxwings.

• Northern evergreen coniferous *trees* are shaped to shed snow. Thick and waxy needles are their armor against wind.

• Leathery and hardy, leaves of some evergreen *ferns* stay green all year long.

• Sensing longer daylight hours in spring, *avalanche lilies*, *dogtooth violets*, *skunk cabbages*, and other early bloomers actually melt the snow around them as they breathe and grow. This raises the temperature of the air close by, creating individual microclimates. Hairy stems and leaves trap heat against the plant too.

• South-facing gardens, planted against buildings, can mimic natural microclimates. The building traps the sun's heat, melting the snow close by. *Daffodils*, *snowdrops*, and *crocuses* will cheerfully bloom a few feet from a huge snowbank.

• In northern countries, winter grains, such as *wheat*, are planted in the fall to get a jump start on the next growing season. Snow provides protection and insulation for the seeds that are below the soil surface. Farmers have learned to plant the seeds in fields where there is stubble from the last crop. The leftover stalks act as snow catchers or fences, trapping as much snow cover as possible for added insulation and then water when it melts.

Snowbirds

Each species of bird has a snow policy. They live with snow, avoid it, or completely escape it. For many birds, it's not snow but daylight that determines when and if they migrate. Insect eaters have zero tolerance to zero, when nearly all insects disappear, forcing dependent birds south. Ptarmigans, year-round residents of snow country, turn white and blend in with their snowy environment. Chickadees pile into woodpecker holes and huddle together to keep warm. Whatever their policy – stay or leave – birds are well adapted to the phenomenon of snow.

Ptarmigans

Not only do these birds turn white for perfect snow camouflage, but ptarmigans have firm bristlelike feathers on their feet that function like snowshoes while insulating them from the snow.

Spruce Grouse

During blizzards and severe cold snaps, spruce grouse torpedo themselves into fluffy snowbanks and create a cave at the end of a tunnel. Here they wait out the storm in relative comfort. When they climb out, extra scales on their feet improve their traction in snow.

Snow Geese

The main connection between snow geese and snow is the color white. At the first sign of winter, enormous flocks of snow geese migrate to eastern, western, or southern coastal American marshlands, where they overwinter. Each spring they return to the Canadian tundra, timing their arrival with the melting of snow and the exposure of tender young marsh plants, their preferred food source.

Chickadees

When trees are bare, snow is deep, and the sky is threatening, you don't expect to see wildlife. But these conditions don't bother the chickadees. They plan ahead, like red squirrels, caching seeds in the bark of trees for the leaner days of winter. Frequent visitors to bird feeders, chickadees carefully select the fattest and best seeds. And, at night, when their body temperature drops, chickadees must wake up and shake themselves until they have warmed up.

Gray Jays

Gray jays, relatives of the raven, are food storage specialists. Their little brains can remember thousands of hiding places. And gray jays' saliva has a gluelike quality, allowing them to stick seeds high up in trees, well above the snow.

Cardinals

Like most birds, cardinals shiver to keep warm when they are resting. And their feathers can be warmer than the hair of mammals. By fluffing up their feathers, cardinals not only appear to double in size, but they also create air pockets that act as insulation.

Common Poorwills

Members of the goatsucker family, these birds are thought to actually hibernate for short periods of time. As insect eaters, they live where insects usually survive year-round. But, during sudden cold spells, they find shelter and enter a resting state called torpor. Their body temperature drops close to freezing and they appear dead. When conditions improve, they warm up and resume living normally.

Downy Woodpeckers

Downy woodpeckers, and their bigger relative the hairy woodpecker, don't migrate. They excavate holes in dead trees, both for shelter and in search of insects and insect eggs. A feeder with sunflower seeds or suet attracts these woodpeckers. Fat helps them survive blizzards and cold.

Snowy Owls

True snowbirds, snowy owls live in the open. Thickly feathered from their beaks to their toes, they keep warm, even near the North Pole. When they migrate, it's for food, not to avoid snow or cold. They eat lemmings and, when the lemming population drops, the owls head south to find food.

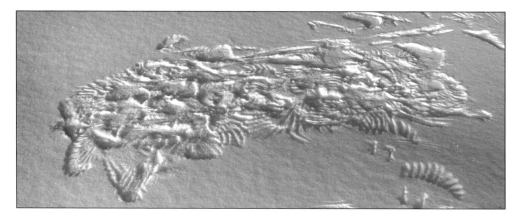

Gyrfalcons

The largest of all falcons, gyrfalcons can be as white as snow or dark as a thundercloud. Living year-round in the most northerly parts of the world, these predators are adapted to hunting on windy snow-swept landscapes, specializing in killing ptarmigans. It's not their color that helps them with the hunt, but their amazing speed.

Ravens

Kwack! Kwack! The hoarse croak of a raven rebounds around the forest, letting all know he's found a carcass. That's how ravens thrive in cold, snowy, and remote habitats – by their sharp wit and opportunistic nature. Before meat freezes or becomes covered with snow, ravens have staked it out, filled their bellies, and carted off and cached morsels for later.

Snow Buntings

First autumn sightings of snow buntings mean snow is on the way for central North America. In winter, flocks of snow buntings swoop around snow-swept fields, searching for grain leftovers and weed seeds. Nesters of the high Arctic, they arrive in early spring, when snow remains everywhere, letting local people know that winter is nearly over.

Snow Mammals

Snow-Adapted Moose

These thirteen road hockey players form the general length and weight (600 kg or 1323 lbs.) of an adult male moose. But none are as tall (2 m or 6.5 ft.). In fact, some players could likely fit under a moose's belly. And half the team would be needed to hold up its massive rack of antlers, which are 2 meters (6.5 ft.) across and weigh about 30 kilos (66 lbs.). Facing a blizzard head-on, you'd rather be a big strong moose than one hockey player. Size, weight, and strength help moose have an average life span of twenty-seven winters.

Like many mammals that prefer cold climates, moose have special adaptations for surviving the northern forests' eight-month winters. Fat stores, packed on during the summer, add insulation under their dense fur, and moose are warm through the coldest storms. Their large hooves give a solid grip on ice and some types of snow. And their long legs prance through drifts and give them a leg up on other herbivores as they reach vegetation high up in trees. Amazingly flexible necks and rough tongues allow them to grab and snap off hard-to-reach twigs. During heavy snowstorms, moose seek shelter under the canopy of mature trees, nibbling on twigs until the weather clears. Moose eat between 15 and 20 kilos (33 to 44 lbs.) of twigs and shrubbery each winter's day.

Preferring temperatures under 15° C (60° F), moose regularly cool off in lakes on hot summer days. Global warming is threatening moose habitat by raising temperatures, reducing snowfalls, and shortening winters. The warmer climate has also increased the range of white-tailed deer. They're moving north into moose territory, bringing with them a brain parasite deadly to moose. But, even more lethal are wolves. Few moose die of old age; most end up in the bellies of wolves.

Wolves – Seasoned Moose Hunters

When wolves swallow their last gulp of food, they begin looking for their next meal. Moose – a primary winter food source that's at least three times the size of the largest wolf – fight ferociously for their lives. A well-aimed front hoof can break bones, or even finish off a reckless wolf. But one in ten hunts is successful, usually taking the very old moose or young calf. Wolves are cunning hunters that rely on stealthy attacks and planned ambushes. They aren't good long-distance runners and moose can outrun them, especially in snow. But wolves have learned to stalk and pounce or chase a moose towards waiting members of their pack. Sometimes, in heavy snow conditions, a moose becomes mired down. Then wolves will nip at its legs until blood loss and exhaustion result, and they move in for the kill.

Chipmunks – Winter Haters

Chipmunks avoid the cold and snow in underground burrows dug below tree roots or rotting stumps. But they don't sleep through winter like groundhogs. Instead, they waken every few days, eat nuts and seeds from their cache, pass a little urine and a few droppings, and go back to sleep. Rolled in snug balls with their noses tucked under their tails, thick fur keeps chipmunks warm between snacks.

Porcupines – Armored Snowplows

Porcupines have winter survival down to a science. They're slow moving, so they don't waste energy. They eat almost any plant life – from bullet-hard bark to sticky pine needles. And they sleep anywhere – in trees, under rock piles, or inside an abandoned cabin. They are practically perfect snow creatures.

Thirty thousand sharp quills on their backs and tails protect porcupines from most predators. Fishers, coyotes, and great horned owls strike porcupines from the front, aiming for the head or underbelly. But a miss can mean death to the attacker. Porcupine quills are designed to dig in and fester. Where they don't have quills, porcupines have woolly fur with long guard hairs that keep them warm throughout cold snowy winters.

Deep snow never stopped a hungry porcupine. Nocturnal most of the year, porcupines feed night and day in winter. They plow their way to the nearest tree, clamber above the snow, and methodically strip off all the bark. Coarse hard hairs assist porcupines to grip the tree bark, while their hind feet clamp onto branches. Both these adaptations help them climb and hold on while feeding, even in wind and blowing snow.

Porcupines occupy a small territory in winter – foraging within 100 m (328 ft.) of shelter. They wait out snow or rain up in a tree, but are smart enough to stay in their dens during blizzards. Solitary most of the year, porcupines – like voles, mice, and shrews – snuggle up and share body heat during severe winter weather. Up to one hundred porcupines have been found sheltering in one rock pile.

Red Squirrels – Winter Lovers

Red squirrels live nearly everywhere in the global northern forest. Active on cold and bleak days, like the porcupine they take to their nests only in the worst blizzards. Weighing less than a large potato, they survive by scurrying along evergreen branches, scolding all intruders, eating, and keeping their heart rates up. And, they've planned for winter. Their primary activity all year long is searching for and caching food. While they prefer seeds from cones, they'll eat other seeds, nuts, insects, eggs, smaller fellow
rodents, and even the bark off conifers. Red squirrels know they'll lose some food to scavengers, so they store it in many hiding spots – some is buried underground, some under leaves or fallen logs, some in the crotches of tree branches. They hang mushrooms to dry and then bury them. The bulk of their winter food stores is often found in a large midden, or heap, near their nest. Added to year after year, these middens can be several meters in diameter. If you approach one in the woods, expect a grumpy red squirrel to chitter, stamp its feet, and flick its tail menacingly. Not scary for you, but threatening enough to make some creatures back off.

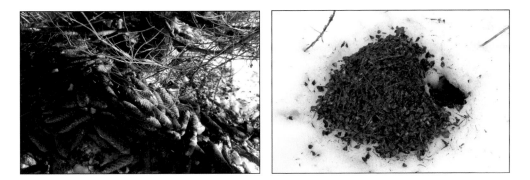

Red squirrels are true tree squirrels, but know how to use snow-covered ground to their advantage. Below their tree nests, they dig extensive tunnels leading to their food middens and to safe sheltered spots on the snow surface where they can assess the weather and the world. Some tunnels lead conveniently to the base of a well-stocked bird feeder. On fair days, red squirrels make countless trips back to their nests, cheeks bulging with seeds.

Caribou Winter

Gilbert Flowers carves herds of delicate, hand-sized caribou out of birch and bone. He catches each animal in a slightly different pose, so when they are together the herd comes alive. The caribou look as if they are jostling, nodding, sniffing, and nudging each other as they trot along with their easy, leg-swinging gait. Their hooves, at first glance, look oversized and cartoonlike. But Gilbert, from Hopedale, Labrador, knows caribou well and carves them in perfect proportion.

Caribou, and their reindeer next of kin, have feet superbly adapted for surviving in snow country. Their snowshoe hooves help bear their weight on top of deep snow. The normally unused dewclaw – found higher up the foot in most deer, dogs, and pigs – is well developed in caribou and splays on snow to add even more width to each hoof. The front of the hoof has a sharp edge for traction on ice and for breaking through crust to enable caribou to eat lichens. In winter, the pads under each hoof harden and grow dense oily bristles between the toes to protect the area from scratches and from clogging with ice and snow. And a tendon in the hoof makes a loud snap or click as caribou walk, so an individual can keep up with the herd, even in a blizzard.

Caribou are not only built for snow, they also seem to have snow sense. Look for caribou in winter and you'll usually find them feeding where the snow is no more than 65 cm (2 ft.) deep and just the right softness for digging trenches to find their preferred food, lichen. If the snow gets too deep or too hard after a snowstorm or melt, caribou move on – even if they have to travel hundreds of kilometers. They go wherever walking is easier – along ridges, where the snow is thinner, or across lakes, where the snow is harder – to reach snow that is just right for digging and grazing again. At night, or when they have finished feeding, they move out of the forest and onto frozen lakes or ridges where they can see and outrun their enemies – wolves or people. In some areas, caribou eat lichens that grow on trees, but again, they look for the right amount and hardness of snow to hold their weight as they stand under the trees.

In many places, caribou are becoming scarce. Global warming is a major threat. Midwinter thaws followed by refreezing can turn soft snow into crust too hard for even a caribou hoof to break. Almost all the endangered Peary caribou of the Canadian Arctic starved to death in 1995 because their lichen was covered with thick ice. Meanwhile, clear-cut logging, pipeline construction, snowmobiling, heli-skiing, and other human activities alter snow depth and softness in southern caribou country. The animals sense changes and often will not cross disturbed areas, even if there is food and safety on the other side. Elegantly adapted to live in wild snowy places, caribou are in danger of disappearing with their natural snow habitat.

Gilbert's people are working to set aside large wild areas where the land, snow, and caribou are left untouched. His carvings remind us that caribou are magnificent, but their future fragile.

Snow Ecology: Studying Life under the Snow

Snow ecologists are a small dedicated group of scholars who study the science of snow. They are intrigued by snow as a habitat and are not afraid to dig right in and bury themselves in their work. No temperature-controlled classrooms for this hardy lot. Their laboratories are out in the elements. Unlike city dwellers who fight snow all winter long, snow ecologists befriend the cool world between the ground and the snow crust.

Frank Salisbury

Frank Salisbury drives his snowmobile deep into the forest wilderness of Utah. What's a plant specialist doing here in winter? He's monitoring how plants buried under snow adapt to the ups and downs of winter cold. Underground, he constructed a steel "greenhouse," where he measures the growth of seedlings and the amount of light that filters through the deep snow.

W.O. Pruitt

W.O. Pruitt's fascination with snow has earned him the name Dr. Snow. He uses many specific snow words of the Kovakmiut of Alaska (see page 11) to describe the survival of boreal wildlife, particularly the woodland caribou and vole. His favorite snow is pukak, the delicate crystal underside of the snowpack. Pukak is where species such as spiders, insects, voles, and weasels endure the winter and where lichen thrives. As Dr. Snow says, "You have to get down on your belly . . . with a magnifier and light reflector in order to appreciate pukak."

Bernd Heinrich

Bernd Heinrich describes himself as a "hunter of winter marvels." He tramps the woods of Maine, pokes his nose into crossbill nests, follows the cries of ravens to their carrion feasts, listens for the sweet tweets of kinglets, and bangs on trees, searching for flying squirrel nests. He asks a lot of questions. For example, why do red squirrels throw away some pinecones and eat others? After close examination, Heinrich concludes that the squirrels eat only fully packed pinecones and toss aside those that have few seeds. Wasting precious energy in winter can cost a creature its life.

Joy Finlay

For Joy Finlay, teacher of winter science and snowshoeing, snow is the right stuff. It protects plants and small creatures from freezing and signals the time for outdoor fun. Only in snow can she find the "black-dot-phenomenon." That's when the sun's warmth attracts adult snow fleas to the surface from the pukak layer below. Thousands, even millions, of insects the size of black pepper grains flip-flop on the sunny snow. Looking closer, she knows she'll find hungry spiders too. Snow fills Joy with wonder and mystery. She's been awarded Canada's top honor – the Order of Canada – for sharing her enthusiasm and knowledge of snow ecology with thousands of students. Coincidentally, the Order's symbol is a perfect, six-sided snowflake.

The Hunters Who Overslept – A Ket's Tale

The first snow of winter crunches under the boots of Novik and Evai, two Ket hunters, as they head north from their Siberian village. With winter closing in, they need meat and furs for their families. All day long they set traplines for ermine and sable, while shooting game along the way. Dusk is falling before they realize how far they've ventured from home.

"Let's camp in the forest for the night," suggests Novik.

"We'll need a fire," replies Evai, eyeing an angry sky, "and shelter."

Rushing to beat the dark and the approaching snowstorm, they gather firewood. Tucked under the base of an old spruce tree, Novik discovers a bear's den.

"Look Evai," he shouts, "we'll be cozy here tonight. There're no tracks in the snow or fresh claw marks on this tree. I think the bear has moved on."

Together they look closer and agree they've stumbled upon the perfect spot for a night in the bush. They build a big fire just beyond the den's opening and prepare a delicious meal of roasted fresh meat, hot tea, and a few dried berries from home. When the flames die to embers, they climb inside the den. The ground is soft, with layers of dry grass, and there's just enough space for two sleepy people. Evai stuffs his fur coat into the entrance and together they climb under Novik's coat. Listening to the storm's increasing might, they feel safe and content, agreeing that the bear had made a good home.

"I hope he's warm in his new lair," murmurs Evai, as they drift into deep sleep.

Brilliant light is peeking around the edges of the entrance when Novik wakes up. He elbows Evai, saying, "The storm's over, but there must be tons of snow. Look how bright it is outside."

Together they tug aside Evai's coat and clamber into the open. Rubbing their eyes in amazement, they see no snow at all. And the sun is high in the sky. "What's this?" wonders Novik. "The sun is confusing winter. It thinks it's spring!"

The two hunters hurry towards home, mystified by the sights around them. Their dogs rush out to greet them, but howl and bark wildly as they circle and sniff.

"This may sound strange," says Evai, "but I don't think the dogs recognize us."

Novik's children peer out of his tent, and then disappear. Seconds later his wife bursts from the tent, screeching and calling his name. Alarmed, people in neighboring tents, Evai's family, in fact the entire village come running. Between hugs and kisses, Novik looks at his son, visibly taller than when he saw him last. He bursts out laughing. "We've slept like bears all winter long. It really *is* spring."

From this day forward, Ket hunters always stay clear of bear dens. Who wants to sleep away the winter? And which hunter can afford losing a winter's catch?

Migration, Hibernation, or Celebration

At Home in the Snow

Your forehead stings, your fingertips are numb, and your nose hairs clump together when you breathe. Clear sky, still air, crunching snow under your feet – what a frigid January afternoon! Your body tells you that, come night, the black sky will drain away any heat left in the air. The temperature may drop to forty below.

Where would you like to spend the evening? Deep in an upholstered chair, snuggled in a warm blanket, facing a glowing fire, one hand reaching for a cup of steaming hot chocolate; or constructing a shelter out of snow that will help you, if you are careful, survive the night?

Most people prefer to get away from the cold. They construct insulated wood, brick, or stone houses and carefully protect their doorways from wind and blowing snow. No matter how severe the storm outside, indoors becomes a refuge for rainforest plants, tropical fish, and warm-weather humans.

However, some hardy people invent ways to stay warm, even through the worst cold, by constructing shelters out of snow. They use the insulating properties of snow to keep the heat from draining away. At the same time, they are in touch with the snowy world they live in.

Igloo

The Inuit invented a snow house that takes two people a few hours to build and can last much of the winter. Builders look for wind-packed tundra snow, preferably deposited in one snowstorm. Using a long snow knife or saw, they cut blocks of snow from the area where the inside living space will be. Each block is about as long as a person's arm, as thick as the width of an outstretched hand, and shaved so the top side is on an angle. The blocks are placed in a circle and, because the top sides are angled, rise in a spiral to form a dome. The builders work inside the circle for most of the construction, moving outside to chink in gaps with snow and to drop the final keystone block into the top of the dome.

With a couple of candles and the entrance closed with a block of snow, the inside of an igloo will stay just below freezing while the outside temperature

may dip under forty below. In a sleeping bag, a person can sleep comfortably inside an igloo.

Quinzhee

People who live south of the tundra invented a cavelike shelter made out of softer forest snow. It takes two people a couple of hours to build, but a quinzhee lasts only a few nights. Builders need just 15 cm (6 in.) of snow, but, unlike an igloo, layered snow from different storms works best.

Snow is tossed in the air with a shovel or broad end of a snowshoe and piled to form a mound about 2 m (6.5 ft.) high. It is left to settle, harden, or sinter for over an hour. Then a small hole is cut into the side and a room dug out of the center. A snow roof should be left, no more than 30 cm (1 ft.) thick, with at least one ventilation hole poked through for fresh air. Usually the excavation hole is filled in and a small entrance cut at ground level at ninety degrees to the wind. Inside, the temperature stays below freezing, but much warmer than outside. Although unlikely to collapse, people who lie or sleep in quinzhees should keep a shovel beside them so they can dig their way out if necessary.

Why Dress for Snow?

Here's the challenge. You can wear anything – as many layers as you like – but when the blizzard hits, stand with the musk oxen and see who gets cold first.

Ridiculous! There is no clothing that can keep you as warm as a musk ox in a blizzard. Cold and snow will eventually cut through the most deluxe snowsuit.

Outside, without protection from the wind, you'll eventually freeze solid. The musk ox, on the other hand, is the only creature that can literally stand firm through a raging snowstorm. It wears two coats – a fine wool undercoat, overlaid by a coarse outer coat that nearly touches the ground. Ears, nose, and tail are all under cover of the best wool in the world. That's why musk oxen live where there's snow ten months of the year and some of the coldest temperatures ever recorded.

Humans are best suited to life in the Tropics, and need clothing and shelter to survive everywhere else. If you jump into a snowbank in your bathing suit, unlike a musk ox, your body can't cope with the cold in snow. Without blubber, a thick hide, or fur, the human body undergoes these reactions to cold and snow:

• *Goose bumps* – At the first sign of cold, goose bumps appear on your cool flesh, causing fine skin hairs to stand up and bristle. Soon after, your body shakes with shivers.

• *Chilblains* – Linger in the snow for more than a few minutes and chilblains can develop – a painful swelling or hot red itchy skin. Seek shelter and there'll be no permanent damage, as most skiers and skaters know from experience.

• *Frost Nip* – You're getting close to frostbite when your skin stiffens and turns as red as a bad sunburn. The flesh under the skin remains soft and doesn't blister. At this point, the body starts to redirect blood from the arms, legs, and face to keep the vital organs working, making fingers, toes, ears, and nose tingle.

• *Superficial Frostbite* – Next, skin turns a bluish white and begins to freeze and harden. Emergency medical treatment is urgently needed before deep frostbite sets in.

• *Deep Frostbite* – When the winter's cold permeates deep into the flesh, it often damages tissue beyond repair. American explorer Robert Peary lost eight toes to frostbite trying to reach the North Pole.

• *Hypothermia* – If the normal core body temperature of 37°C (98.6°F) drops below 31° C (88° F), you lose consciousness. If your temperature continues to drop to 24° C (75° F), death usually occurs. That's the air temperature of a warm spring day.

Bundle up

Becoming extremely cold can have grave consequences. Northerners and winter sports enthusiasts have learned that dressing in layers, wearing wool, changing wet clothing, and paying attention to their body's signals makes good sense.

Snow Travel

With only two long legs and rather narrow feet, humans are not well adapted for walking in snow, especially deep snow. But by using our brainpower, we have invented ways to travel over snow.

Snowshoes and skis

The idea of enlarging the human foot to walk on top of snow surfaced in Asia more than 5,000 years ago. Eurasians developed skis while North Americans perfected snowshoes. Over the centuries, both inventions were modified for local conditions. Skiers in mountainous areas, for instance, learned to pull fur socks onto their skis to walk uphill without slipping backwards. Snowshoers crafted frame and mesh to suit their region's kind of snow – a round bear paw design for dense thick snow and a narrow turned-up-toe frame with fine netting for light fluffy snow.

Komatiks and toboggans

About 7,000 years ago, Siberians invented the dogsled for moving cargo across snow. The Inuit refined it and created the komatik, a light rugged sled with runners. When hitched to dogs pulling side by side in a fan formation, the komatik can speed across wind-hardened tundra snow.

Aboriginal people of the boreal forest region south of the tundra invented the toboggan, made from birch cut along the grain. With turned-up-toe tips and no runners, toboggans float on soft fluffy forest snow. And when hitched to dogs harnessed in a line, a toboggan can weave smoothly through bush.

The Sami of Scandinavia invented the pulka, a snow boat with runners, which hooks up easily behind reindeer. Modern search and rescue personnel use a modified pulka as a stretcher to move the injured across snow.

Snow machines

V.D. Wright of New Hampshire invented the first motorized over-snow vehicle in 1913 when he put a Ford car on skis and replaced the rear wheels with cleated belts. In 1922, at age fifteen, Canadian Armand Bombardier built his first snowmobile from a Model T and a sleigh. Other inventors tried powering toboggans or sleds with motorcycle, combine, trac-

tor, and even washing machine motors. In 1937, Bombardier patented a drive sprocket and track, leading the way to the mass production of his Ski-Doo in 1959.

Meanwhile, inventors worked with tractors, skis, and treads to make larger, heavy-duty over-snow machines for logging and the oil industry. Eventually their ideas were used to develop snow groomers for ski resorts.

Snow in the city

At the end of January 1999, after a month of frequent snowfall with little melt, two big snowstorms hit the city of Toronto. The mayor declared a state of emergency and called in the army. People who lived outside the city scorned the mayor's actions – they were used to more snow than Toronto ever had. But in a city of millions of people dependent on travel by car, truck, and bus on clear roads, deep snow creates serious safety hazards.

Inventors have patented many ways to rid city streets of snow. There are dozens of different kinds of snow shovels – one even patented by a woman named Fairweather. But no matter how many shovels, plows, blowers, or melters a city owns, one blizzard can defeat them all, paralyze traffic, and endanger citizens. That's when people should cross their long legs, put up their narrow feet, and sit out a big city snowstorm.

The Summer of Snow – A Gitksan Legend

Have you ever wished that winter was over and the snow all gone? In this old story from northern British Columbia, a whole community suffers because one young man called out to the sky, complaining loudly about wintry weather.

In spring, the Gitksan would cross the great river and set out their fish traps. One year, their traps filled immediately with beautiful salmon. As was the custom, their chief cleaned and cooked them. Then the young men and women of his household carried a platter to each family in the village.

As they delivered the fish, cold gray clouds swept overhead and hailstones beat the ground. Deelepzeb, a young man in line to be chief, looked up and, shaking his head, called out, "What is the meaning of this? What stupidity! How can it hail in salmon season!"

Deelepzeb thought no more of his rant, but several people had heard him and thought him foolish to speak rudely to the sky spirits.

That night it started to snow and continued snowing for days. The snow piled so high that hunters couldn't travel into the bush for fresh meat, wild food plants were buried, and the river froze so solid that no one could fish. As it was still springtime, food supplies in the village were low and people began to starve. Finally there was no food left at all.

Deelepzeb was one of the first to grow sick from hunger. His two sisters pulled him on a sled down the river ice to look for food. After traveling for many hours, they set up camp but found nothing to eat. Too weak to continue, Deelepzeb died.

As the sisters prepared his body for cremation, a little parcel fell from his clothes onto the snow. In it they found half a dried salmon – enough to have saved him. Sadly, they sang a lament for their brother. Then they broke the fish into pieces and ate it, a little at a time, to keep from dying themselves.

When they ran out of food again, the sisters broke camp and traveled farther downriver on ice and through deep snow. As they trudged along, they started to feel a warm scented breeze on their faces. Then more heat rolled towards them in waves. Excited, thinking the weather was about to change, they walked faster. But instead of a weather change, they came to a place where the snow just stopped and the land opened ahead in full, lush, late summer. They looked back – all behind was locked in snow.

The exact place where snow gave way to summer was the edge of the territory of the Gitksan. The sisters realized that their people alone were suffering with snow and freezing cold. Then they remembered their brother's foolish taunt to the sky spirits.

Ahead in the summer sunshine, a blue jay flew by carrying a cluster of red elderberries. One sister spotted a ripe crab apple growing on a rosebush, picked it, and shared it with the other. They sat, ate, and sang another lament, telling the sad story of their brother's death, their people's punishment, and their own survival.

People's Choice – Vacate, Vegetate, or Celebrate

Are you a -phobe, a -phore, or a -phile? More than fifty years ago, Alexander Formozov, the grandfather of snow ecology, studied the way species responded to a snow environment and divided them into three categories: chionophobes – snow avoiders, chioneuphores – snow endurers, and chionophiles – snow lovers. These categories apply to mammals, plants, birds, and bugs, and they apply to you too. How would you classify yourself – someone who vacates, vegetates, or celebrates during the season of snow?

Vacate

Most people don't have the option to leave snow behind and head south. School, family, work, and extracurricular activities bind them to one place.

Nomadic peoples, such as Sami and Nenet reindeer herders in northern Scandinavia and Siberia, follow their herds from summer calving grounds on the treeless tundra to winter shelter in the trees of the boreal forest. The move means reindeer can find their own food and together herders and deer spend winter in a less harsh environment.

Snowbirds – northerners who spend the winter in the sunny South – completely avoid snow and winter. Senior citizens flock to trailer parks, condos, and other vacation hot spots. If you're someone who spends winter dreaming of warmer climates, collects travel brochures of places with sand and palm trees, and shivers at the thought of going outside, you're a chionophobe or snowbird in the making.

Vegetate

Snow can be blamed for creating an entire subgroup of human beings – couch potatoes. Adopting the equivalent of torpor in birds, these people choose to spend the winter reading books, watching TV, playing computer games, baking cookies, talking on the phone – anything but making contact with snow. They don't own skates, skis, toboggans, or snowboards and go outdoors only when absolutely necessary.

Winter can make chioneuphores suffer from seasonal affective disorder, cabin fever, flu, and the winter blahs. If you spend the winter cocooning indoors with the heat cranked up and hot chocolate on standby, you're in this category. You'll perk up when you hear "spring is just around the corner."

Celebrate

A recent random survey shows chionophiles answered these questions identically:

Favorite

word: snow

knickknack: snow dome

color: white

season: winter

weather: blizzard

treat: snow cone

song refrain: "Let it snow, let it snow, let it snow."

But chionophiles are not all the same. They have unique and different ways of celebrating snow:

Dogsled racing

Harnessed and ready for the four-mile run, four Alaskan huskies leap forward to the command *hup, hup, hup!* Tongues flapping and blue eyes on the trail ahead, these canine athletes thrill their musher (driver) with a record time. The sled dogs are rewarded with hugs, kisses, and a real doggie massage. Their owners could take home $25,000 in prize money, but they travel to Minden from all over North America for the six feet of fresh snow, reunion with old friends, fabulous food, and the carnival setting of this small Ontario town. And, to win in dogsledding, all that matters is how you steer your sled.

Winter golf

If golf's your sport, why let a little snow and cold delay the game? Every year die-hard golfers have a February tee off in Harrison, Michigan with mascot Frost Bite Bear cheering them on. Warm-ups for the Frost Bite Open include sled decorating and longest-ball driving contests. Do they use white golf balls?

Downhill skiing

Forty-five hundred years ago, skiers in Sweden hunted game by gliding over the snow on wide short skis. Forty-three hundred years later, skiing became a sport, with the first organized jumping, downhill, and cross-country competitions occurring in the early 1800s. Now there are millions of skiers worldwide. From Olympic racers to backyard ski-bunnies doing the snowplow, skiers are total chionophiles.

Snowshoeing

Snowshoes are the ultimate off-road vehicles for extreme or mellow chionophiles. With a set of ski poles for extra stability, you can explore wild places that aren't even accessible in summer. Or you can take a leisurely snowshoe by moonlight, savor a winter picnic, and look for Sasquatch or an owl's nest.

Arctic winter games

Frost clings to the parkas of northern athletes and their boots squeak on the snow as the outdoor parade marks the beginning of the circumpolar games. There are the familiar skiing and hockey competitions, along with snowsnake, snowshoeing, and dogsledding. Indoors sports – knuckle hopping, finger pulling, and high kicking – stress skills of strength and endurance traditionally performed in the small space of a snow house.

Snow sculpture

Ack! Hours of snow shoveling ahead of you? Artist Mark Thurman saw a dragon in a mountain of snow and cleared a path while creating a sparkling sculpture. The serpent's tail rested at the back door; its body wound around the porch railing and post; its front legs clung to the edge of the stairs as its head lunged into the yard. A menacing tongue and frosty fire failed to melt the snow.

The Birds' Lacrosse Game
– An Ojibwa Legend

Before a fateful game of lacrosse, there was no winter. This Ojibwa legend tells how Loon's love of lacrosse and a foolhardy bet brought cold and snow to the north, changing the lives of birds – and all creatures – forever.

Loon was obsessed with lacrosse. But the other birds were bored with it and refused to play. Loon was convinced he could change their minds, so he started with Raven. He mocked the proud black bird, claiming his lacrosse

team could whip the feathers off Raven's. Raven laughed in Loon's face and flew away.

Loon tried a different angle with Hawk, asking her sweetly to please play lacrosse. Hawk was flattered, but worried the day was too hot. Loon suggested they play in the cool of the next morning, and he offered Hawk first choice of players. Loon was so agreeable that Hawk became suspicious and nearly canceled the match.

"A bet! Let's make a bet!" blurted Loon. "If your team wins, you decide on a penalty for my team. If mine wins, you must play lacrosse whenever I ask."

Hawk liked this plan and immediately chose Raven for her team. Loon selected Kingbird. Hawk nabbed Woodpecker and Grouse – both hardy birds. Loon chose Oriole and Catbird – clever players. When the teams were complete, Loon and Hawk agreed the game would start at sunrise and end with the first goal.

The next morning the captains assigned positions – Hawk put Woodpecker in goal; Loon chose Oriole. Right from the start, Loon's team looked stronger. It was fast and aggressive, but couldn't score. As the players jostled in front of Woodpecker's net, Grouse tried stealing the ball from Catbird, but hit him by mistake. Catbird lost his balance and sent Raven squawking to the ground. Catbird saw his chance and flung another shot at Woodpecker. As the ball flew over Raven's head, Raven jumped up and snatched it. He streaked down the field and flicked the ball past Oriole and into the net. The game was over.

"Loon," said Hawk fiercely, "this is your penalty. Whenever the wind blows from the east, rain, thunder, and lightning will prevent you from playing lacrosse."

The crowd gasped but Loon yelled back, "Cheaters! You cheated so the bet's off. We'll play again tomorrow. Same bet but Vulture will referee. Let's see if you can win fairly."

The second game began at dawn. Again, Loon's team battered Woodpecker with shots. Woodpecker blocked the ball with his wings, feet, and head. By late afternoon Loon's team was tired and couldn't control the ball until Kingbird intercepted a pass. As he raced back towards Woodpecker, Raven stuck out his foot, tripping Kingbird. Raven snatched up the loose ball, sprinted towards Oriole, and slid the ball into the net.

Loon's team shouted at Vulture to call a foul. But Vulture hadn't seen Raven trip Kingbird, so declared the goal fair. All eyes turned to Hawk.

"Loon, this your penalty. When the north wind blows, temperatures will freeze and snow will fall. All the birds on your team will migrate south."

As Hawk flew off, a gust of cold air swirled round from the north – the penalty had started. From that day on, Loon and his teammates were chased away with the first snow of each winter, unable to return until spring.

For Snow's Sake

Snow-covered land is an amazing habitat. It shelters the earth and provides a home for living things – from microscopic snow algae to spiders, tulip bulbs, chipmunks, bears, and people. In winter, active animals – such as birds, mice, and deer – eat snow to get water. Snowmelt renews soil, fills rivers and ponds, and awakens dormant seeds and plants in springtime. And while snow has little nutritional value, it hosts a banquet of edibles from its pukak layer to its crust. It's under snow that mice feed on grain and twigs; it's through snow that foxes find mice.

It's not surprising that snow is threatened. Global warming, resulting in climate change, is still a hot topic, but most scientists agree that we are past the warning stages. Polar ice and the northern snow cover are melting. If the current rate continues, scientists expect a dramatic decrease throughout the twenty-first century, making life difficult and eventually impossible for caribou, moose, and polar bear. And the traditional lives of people sharing these habitats will be in jeopardy too. Ice and snow reflect Sun's energy back out into the atmosphere.

As this reflective surface shrinks, increased sunlight will make temperatures rise all around the world, making climate change everyone's problem.

You can keep snow in your future by living "green." The main cause of global warming is human activity – the burning of fossil fuels to power cars, factories, air conditioners, and furnaces. Individual, family, and community reduction of energy use will be like rolling a snowball. Each positive change will help halt and ultimately reverse the increasing temperatures.

Then we won't have to imagine a world without polar bears, wet mitts, snowmen, skiing, snowy owls, blizzards, snow forts, Winter Olympics, dogsleds, Ski-Doos, caribou, snowsuits, cold noses, or hot chocolate!

Glossary

accumulation: buildup, such as layers of snow that build up on the ground over a period of time

adaptations: modifications in the physical form or behavior of a plant or animal that help it survive in its particular environment, e.g., the large hooves of a caribou help it travel on deep snow

air masses: vast bodies of air that can cover several thousand square kilometers (or miles) to a height of several kilometers (over a mile). The temperature and moisture remain steady across any one horizontal layer.

avalanches: large masses of snow, ice, earth, or rock that suddenly break loose from a slope and slide downhill

blizzards: violent winter storms that last at least three hours with below-freezing temperatures, very strong winds, and blowing snow, reducing visibility to less than 1 km (1/2 mi.)

cairns: stones heaped into piles to create landmarks

camouflage: the body-covering a plant or animal uses to blend in to its surroundings, e.g., the brown summer feathers of a ptarmigan turn white in winter to blend with the snow

chioneuphores: snow tolerators such as animals that survive in snow and endure winter by changing the way they live (e.g., moose, wolves, voles)

chionophiles: snow lovers such as animals well suited to live in snow with winter-white coloring, snowshoelike feet, etc. (e.g., ptarmigans, lynx, snowy owls)

chionophobes: snow haters such as animals poorly adapted to snow (e.g., house cats, snakes, certain songbirds)

climate: the usual and expected weather of a region averaged over many years

crampons: metal spikes worn on boots to prevent slipping and to aid climbing on snow and ice

crevasses: long and deep cracks in glacial ice

crystals, ice: six-sided ice needles, columns, or plates that form when cooled water vapor molecules hit tiny particles of dust in the atmosphere. Ice crystals can branch and grow in size by absorbing more water vapor until they become heavy enough to fall to the ground as **snow crystals**.

crystallization: the process of forming solid crystals, as when water vapor (gas) turns directly to ice (solid) without going through the liquid phase (water). See **sublimation**.

dehydration: the extreme loss or removal of water from a body

dormant: in a sleeplike state where all activity slows down and growth stops. Often used to describe the inactivity of plants in winter.

ecologists, snow: biologists who study the inter-action of all the living and nonliving parts of a snowy environment

fronts: zones where **air masses** of different temperatures and carrying different amounts of moisture meet. The leading edge of an advancing cold air mass is called a cold front and the leading edge of a warm air mass is called a warm front.

glaciers: large, long-lasting accumulations of snow that form on land and flow, very slowly, downhill

global warming: the worldwide trend of increasing average temperatures

hibernation: a deep winter sleep in a confined space during which an animal's vital functions (including heartbeat and breathing) slow down dramatically

insulation: a material that prevents or slows down the leakage or transfer of heat or cold

meteorologists: scientists who study the atmosphere, including weather and climate

microclimate: the climate of a small, usually sheltered, spot that is different from the greater surrounding area

migration: the seasonal movement of animals from one region to another

mirages: optical illusions caused by light traveling through layers of heat in the atmosphere so that an object looks distorted or in a different location than its true position. See **refraction**.

moraines: deposits of soil, gravel, and rock that build up beside, in front of, or underneath glaciers

nomadic: without a fixed pattern or permanent home, moving from place to place in search of food, often with the change of seasons

pukak: the fragile base layer of snow made up of enlarged, latticelike crystals, sometimes called sugar snow (see p. 11 for more snow terms from the Kovakmiut of Alaska)

refraction: the bending or distortion of light as it passes through layers of the atmosphere. See **mirages, sun dogs**.

runoff: snow and ice that melts into water and then flows or drains downhill and/or downstream

scat: animal droppings

scurvy: a painful, wasting disease caused by a diet lacking in vitamin C, resulting in spongy gums, loose teeth, and bleeding into the skin and mucous membranes

sintering: the process by which snow particles weld together and harden without the presence of water

slush: partly melted or watery snow

snowflakes: clusters of snow crystals that fall from a cloud

snowpack: snow that has built up over at least one winter on uplands or mountain slopes

sublimation: the process of a solid turning to gas, as when ice turns directly to water vapor without going through the liquid phase of water. Can also refer to the process of gas turning directly to a solid. See **crystallization**.

sun dogs: brightly colored spots that can appear on either or both sides of the Sun. Sometimes sun dogs are connected in a huge **halo** that circles the Sun. These optical illusions are caused by sunlight traveling through ice crystals in the atmosphere. See **refraction**.

supercooling: the process of cooling a liquid below its freezing point without it solidifying or crystallizing

terminus: the end of a glacier, also called the toe or snout

torpor: a period of dormancy or sluggishness, brought on by a drop in temperature, in which an animal's heart rate slows down to save energy

water vapor: water as a gas

windchill: not the actual air temperature, but a measurement of what the temperature feels like with the added effect of wind

Index

Photo Credits

Title page: David Love (hereafter DL), Choutla Lake YT; *4-5, all photos*: DL, King ON; *9, left*: Jim Drake (hereafter JMD), Banff AB; *right*: DL, Sedona AZ; *10*: JMD, Markdale ON; *12*: DL, King ON; *13, top*: Ann Love (hereafter AL), Nares Lake YT; *bottom*: DL, King ON; *14*: Bob Lank, Cedar Hill ON; *19*: Henry Barnett (hereafter HB), King ON; *20*: HB, Straits of Belle Isle NL; *21*: Jane Drake (hereafter JD), Markdale ON; *22, top*: JD, Markdale ON; *bottom*: DL, Temagami ON; *23*: DL, King ON; *25*: JD, Markdale ON; *30*: JMD, Oulx, Italy; *33*: Robert Lee, French Glacier AB; *38*: JD, Markdale ON; *42*: HB, King ON; *43, left*: HB, King ON; *right*: DL, King ON; *44, left*: AL, Arrowhead Lake NL; *right*: HB, King ON; *45*: JMD, Markdale ON; *46, top*: DL, Carcross YT; *bottom*: DL, Dawson City YT; *47, top*: HB, King ON; *bottom*: Rob Lewis, Tagish YT; *48, top*: HB, King ON; *bottom*: JD, Markdale ON; *49*: DL, Bowmanville ON; *50*: Dave Gibson, Ottawa ON; *51*: DL, Bowmanville ON; *52*: Brian Drake, Lion's Head ON; *53, top*: Rob Lewis, Whitehorse YT; *bottom left*: DL, King ON; *bottom right*: HB, King ON; *55*: AL, King ON – carvings by Gilbert Flowers, Hopedale NL; *63, top*: JMD, Toronto ON; *bottom*: JMD, King ON; *64, top*: JD, Markdale ON; *bottom*: DL, Whitehorse YT; *65*: JMD, Markdale ON; *68, left*: Ron Dueck, Vancouver Island BC; *right*: DL, King ON; *69*: JD, King ON; *70, left*: HB, King ON; *right*: JMD, King ON; *71, left*: DL, Temagami ON; *right*: AL, Nares Lake YT; *80*: DL, King ON